THE END OF ALL TI

THE END OF ALL THINGS EARTHLY

Faith Profiles of the 1916 Leaders

Edited by **David Bracken**

VERITAS

Published 2016 by
Veritas Publications
7–8 Lower Abbey Street
Dublin 1, Ireland
publications@veritas.ie
www.veritas.ie

ISBN 978 1 84730 680 7
Copyright © the editor and individual contributors, 2016

10 9 8 7 6 5 4 3 2 1

A catalogue record for this book is available from the British Library.

Cover design by Barbara Croatto, Veritas Publications
Printed in the Republic of Ireland by Walsh Colour Print, Kerry

*Veritas books are printed on paper made from the wood pulp of managed
forests. For every tree felled, at least one tree is planted, thereby renewing
natural resources.*

CONTENTS

INTRODUCTION

It is appropriate that the centenary of the 1916 Rising and the Decade of Centenaries, 2012–22 – the National Commemoration Programme has initially concentrated on the period 1912–16 – have been the occasion of much reflection, discussion and debate. The number of volumes published to coincide with the 1916 anniversary is testament to that. The present collection, if somewhat limited in extent, seeks to contribute to that ongoing discussion, exploring the important place of faith in the lives of many of the executed leaders. Hopefully the book inhabits a space between two extremes: the hagiography of the past, on the one hand, in which the leaders underwent a process of 'secular sanctification', to use Daithí Ó Corráin's phrase – although the focus on the sixteen executed men will invariably evoke previous martyrologies; and, on the other hand, a present in which the personal faith story of the 1916 leaders is sometimes forgotten.

As Archbishop Diarmuid Martin has recently observed: 'Each of the leading figures had a personal story of faith which accompanied them along their journey.' Contributors were asked to reflect on the personal faith story or spiritual life of one of the sixteen executed leaders, taking an event or a relationship in that person's life or an item associated with them as a point of departure. Each of the reflections – a series of accessible vignettes – serves as an invitation to the general reader to delve more deeply into the extensive literature documenting the Rising and its seminal significance.

While the personal faith of the executed leaders is the subject of these collected reflections, some observations regarding the problematic question of faith and the Rising more generally are apposite. The foundational event of the Irish Republic was a violent revolution. It was grounded in the belief that Irish freedom could only be won, in the words of Michael O'Hanrahan, by 'the red road of war'. To quote Gearóid Ó Tuathaigh in his piece, entitled 'A Sense of the Religious', some of the exponents of the revolution, notably Patrick Pearse, appropriated the Passion and death of Christ 'as the exemplar for the sacrifice needed (and justified) to redeem the Irish nation'. This 'necessary' sacrifice lead to the deaths of over four hundred people, many of them civilians, during the course of Easter Week. How was this justified? Further, the appropriation of religious concepts by Pearse, Plunkett and others in service of a theology of revolution, together with the associated cult of martyrdom, strike a profoundly discordant note in the world of the twenty-first century, preoccupied by the frightening spectre of religiously motivated violence on a global scale.

In the more recent past, those who espoused the use of violence to further their political agenda visited terrible suffering on the people of this island. In the words of Bishop Pat Storey, Church of Ireland Bishop of Meath and Kildare, in her address at the Arbour Hill commemoration in 2015, 'I am old enough to remember waking up every morning, particularly through the seventies, to death. Every morning ... We reeked of death.' Ó Tuathaigh poses the unavoidable question: 'Did 1916 justify the IRA campaign?'

For his part, Dr William Crean, Bishop of Cloyne, speaking at the Mass for the reinterment of Thomas Kent, acknowledged that 'violence and war are cruel instruments by which to accomplish any human endeavour'. At the same time he recognised that Kent was a person of profound conviction: 'one such man amongst others, women and men who shared his dream ... Thomas chose to give his life in the cause of freedom. He and others thereby sowed the seeds of the flowering of a new political dispensation which would become the Republic of Ireland, of which we are all beneficiaries.'

Although it is beyond the reach of a collection such as this to resolve these tensions, it is important that they are nevertheless acknowledged, in the hope that they might be addressed by persons with the relevant competencies – historians, theologians and others – during the Decade of Centenaries. Gearóid Ó Tuathaigh's concise account, though focused on the person of Pearse and his religious sense, adverts to many issues concerning the Rising more generally that continue to cause perplexity and debate, and serves as a very useful introduction to the volume as a whole.

Leaving aside for a moment the contested legacy of the Rising, the execution of the sixteen leaders is a human tragedy that is played out on an individual level in the stories of the executed men, their families and friends and those who ministered to them: Fr Aloysius Travers, clearly shocked by the execution of James Connolly; Michael Mallin's tortured last testament to his wife, Agnes; Monsignor Patrick Browne haunted by the death of his friend Seán MacDiarmada; the potential of the sculptor Willie Pearse and the youthful Ned

Daly come to naught; leaving the reader with a sense of poignancy and loss.

In the face of that tragedy, many of the condemned men are consoled by the Christian narrative and the practice of the faith in which they were schooled. Others display a remarkably profound, yet simple personal faith, as exemplified by Thomas Kent minutes before his death: 'I hope to see the face of my God.' Or the last words spoken by Seán Heuston: 'Jesus, mercy.'

Side by side with these accounts stand the many acts of faith and friendship occasioned by the circumstances of the Rising – the ministry of the Capuchin friars in Church Street a striking and very moving example. Indeed, Archbishop Diarmuid Martin has expressed the hope that the centenary celebrations will find a space to remember the priests of 1916, recalling moreover the role of the staff at the Pro-Cathedral, which became 'a centre of humanitarian and spiritual concern' during Easter Week. The Capuchins played an important additional part in events, recording and disseminating to the wider public accounts of the leaders' final moments. Fifty years later, Fr Louis O'Kane was engaged in a similar activity: his unique collection of interviews with Volunteer veterans recovers the voices of 1916 from oblivion.

The degree to which the strands of faith and fatherland were interwoven is an understandably uncomfortable reality for a contemporary pluralist Ireland – both for Christian believers and members of the wider society – to the extent that there is striking reticence to acknowledge the fact in the official commemoration of the Rising. The discredited over identification of faith and fatherland aside, there is a certain embarrassment even to admit the importance of personal faith in the leaders' lives. To return again to Ó Tuathaigh: 'The life and conduct of any important figure in the past are invariably viewed through the lens of our present-day values, standards and preoccupations.' However, if the full story of the participants is to be properly told, then it is important not to forget the significant personal, inspirational and consoling dimension of faith in their lives. This collection, however brief, which profiles the executed leaders and aspects of their personal faith experience, represents a contribution to that end. It also serves as a reminder to Christians of every persuasion, that people of faith were – to borrow the words of Bishop Storey at Arbour Hill – 'involved in making our past, and we absolutely need to be involved in shaping our future'.

I

A Sense of the Religious

A SENSE OF THE RELIGIOUS: PATRICK PEARSE AND THE LEADERS OF THE RISING

GEARÓID Ó TUATHAIGH

There is no denying the fact that, as they awaited execution after the court-martials that found them guilty, the leaders of the 1916 Rising showed strong Christian fortitude and welcomed the opportunity of being attended to by priests (in most cases, the Capuchins) and reconciled to God. Even the fervent socialist and supposed atheist, James Connolly, made his Confession and his peace with the Church at the end. Moreover, as details of the personal lives of the leaders became more widely known shortly after their execution, and as reports of the way they carried themselves in defeat and death became common knowledge – from their families, their confessors and, in some instances, the British military personnel who dealt with them – the general public began to judge them more sympathetically. More than that, nationalist opinion began to describe the selfless sacrifice of their own lives for the 'higher cause' of Irish freedom as a kind of martyrdom.

This was especially the case with the austere P. H. Pearse, President of the declared Provisional Government and now identified as the 'leader' of the Rising. Pearse's large body of writings began to be published almost immediately after his execution. The fact that both he and his younger brother, Willie, had been executed, leaving his widowed mother and two sisters to grieve, was especially poignant. But Pearse himself had seen to it that the sacrificial aspect of his death was firmly established in his writings, not least in the late correspondence with his mother. He had, so to speak, prepared the heroic story of his devotion to Ireland and his willingness to pay the ultimate price to redeem Ireland's honour, and had done so in terms (and language) that also underlined the shared circumstances of his mother and of Mary at the foot of the cross.

Pearse's early biographers largely took him at his word, and produced accounts of his life that were almost hagiographic. However, this was but an extreme example of a more general and admiring view of the heroic sacrifice of the leaders of the Rising that became the standard version of these events in nationalist Ireland for almost fifty years afterwards. Dissenting or critical views of Pearse were exceptional and muted. Pearse's mother and sisters kept his memory (and his example) before the public. The children of the schools throughout the state were generally presented (in schoolbooks, in the selections of his literary writings) with the portrait of a heroic role model.

From the mid-1960s there were signs that attitudes were shifting, in part due to changing economic, social and cultural priorities in Irish society, but also prompted by reassessments of the Rising during the fiftieth anniversary in 1966. The outbreak of the Troubles in Northern Ireland, quickly descending into a bloody conflict that lasted thirty years, prompted profound reconsideration within nationalist Ireland of the legacy of the 1916 Rising. Troubling moral and ethical issues emerged – for politicians, historians, polemicists and the public at large – regarding the justification for the use of force in achieving political ends. Did 1916 justify the IRA campaign? Particular attention focused on Pearse, who had hitherto enjoyed iconic status in the established version of the Rising. His later writings advocating rebellion and proclaiming the glory of shedding blood in a just cause (a notion that was not uncommon among many writers who were exhilarated by the rush to arms 'for the nation' at the outbreak of the Great War), came under critical scrutiny.

The heavy use of religious imagery in Pearse's writings – and his pervasive use of Christ's Passion and death to redeem his people as the exemplar for the sacrifice needed (and justified) to redeem the Irish nation – troubled many commentators. In 1972, a Jesuit priest, Fr Francis Shaw (whose own political outlook was unsympathetic to republicanism or Irish separatism), judged Pearse's obsessive comparing of his own self-sacrifice to that of Christ (and of his mother's role and suffering as being akin to Mary's) as blasphemous. A host of studies in recent decades have re-examined different aspects of Pearse's personality, ideas and conduct. While his work as a cultural revivalist, literary man and educationalist continues to attract a favourable verdict from expert commentators, the political writings (notably the more sanguinary and apocalyptic items) have received sharper, more critical appraisal. A more complex version of Pearse has re-emerged from this reassessment.

Pearse's writings (including his correspondence) have been available for study for some time. It is likely that they will be re-examined during the 2016 centenary. The life and conduct of any important figure in the past are invariably viewed through the lens of our present-day values, standards and preoccupations. This will be the case also during 2016. But in any assessment of the religious dimension of Pearse's life and ideas, we should try to 'read' him – notably his writings and his language – in the context of his own time.

II
The End of All Things Earthly

ROGER CASEMENT: ALL FAULTS AND FAILURES BLOTTED OUT

OLIVER RAFFERTY

Roger Casement (1864–1916) remains a somewhat enigmatic figure despite a wealth of scholarship on his life. His inspiring work for human rights in the Congo in 1903 and his devastating report on the Putumayo River atrocities in the Amazon in 1910 and 1911, represent not only a testament to his humanitarianism but also a protest against unbridled human greed and exploitation.

The sufferings he witnessed in Africa and South America touched a deep vein in his personality. In the opinion of Fr Thomas Crotty OP (1867–1930) – chaplain to Irish prisoners of war at Limburg, Hesse, whom Casement was trying to recruit into an Irish Brigade for the Germans – his dispositions reflected a truly Catholic sensibility. Having been arrested on Good Friday 1916 while attempting to land from a German U-boat off the coast of Kerry, Casement was taken to London to stand trial for treason, and, in advance of his court appearance, underwent an intense spiritual struggle.

He formally embraced Catholicism and received his first Holy Communion at the 7 a.m. Mass in Pentonville Prison on 3 August 1916, just before his execution. Refusing the customary last meal, he spent the time after Mass in prayer before he was led to the scaffold. One of the chaplains recorded that Casement died 'with all the faith and piety of an Irish peasant ... [with] contrition and resignation to God's will ...'

Casement wrote in his last letter, 'I shall die in the Catholic Faith, for I accept it fully now. It tells me what my heart sought long in vain ... but I saw it in the face of the Irish.' And he added that he would die in 'hope that God will be with me to the end and that all my faults and failures will be blotted out'. It is impossible to know what Casement is referring to but it was believed in many influential circles that he was a promiscuous homosexual. Extracts from his so-called Black Diaries circulated in London during his trial in June and July 1916 and the accounts there of sexual 'depravity', almost certainly were a factor in the refusal of the British cabinet to commute his death sentence despite immense international pressure.

This is not the place to discuss the authenticity or otherwise of the diaries, about which even today there is scholarly disagreement. But among those who knew of the diaries was Cardinal Francis Bourne (1861–1935), Archbishop of Westminster, who wrote in a private memo that there was 'information on the highest authority that his moral life was deplorable'. As a result, Bourne insisted that before being received into the Catholic Church, Casement should sign a declaration stating that he expressed public sorrow 'for any scandal he may have caused by his acts public or private'. A recent biography of Bourne has mistakenly argued that this was simply asking for the abjuration of heresy, which was common with converts before Vatican II.

Casement refused because it was clear that Bourne intended to make the declaration public and rightly argued that it would be tantamount to confessing that he was guilty of each and every rumour attributed to him in either his public or private life, whether true or false, and clearly he would not be in a position to defend himself. Bourne, who acted as the chief recruiter of Catholic chaplains to the armed forces during World War I, allowed his strong military ties and devotion to king and country to overshadow pastoral concern.

Even at this stage, Casement's spiritual journey was wracked by doubts and Bourne's attitude did not make things easier for him. Father Thomas Carey, the Assistant Chaplain at Pentonville, in whose parish the prison was located, discovered that in addition to being baptised in the Church of Ireland, Casement's mother had three of her four children, including Roger, baptised as Catholics by Fr Felix Poole SJ, during a visit to Rhyl in August 1868. The fact of Casement's Catholic Baptism allowed the chaplain at Pentonville to reconcile Casement to the Church in *articulo mortis* (at the point of death), but Bourne refused to allow Casement to receive the Sacrament of Confirmation.

In his weeks in Brixton and Pentonville Prisons, Casement read such works as *The Imitation of Christ* and biographies of St Francis of Assisi and St Columbanus. Before he died he distributed his few possessions, which included a crucifix, some Rosary beads and a scapular. That he died a true and sincere Catholic there can be no doubt. Yet it is also clear that some forces in institutional Catholicism would have been just as happy if he had not become a Catholic.

Bourne received a rebuke over the Casement affair from no less a person than Cardinal Gaetano de Lai (1853–1928), Camerlengo of the Holy Roman Church. De Lai wrote in December 1916, saying that it had come to his attention that

Bourne had placed conditions on Casement's reconciliation with the Church, requiring him to make a declaration about actions in his public or private life. De Lai remarked that such a thing if true – and were made public – would give scandal. Bourne replied that the allegations were *basée*, or not without foundation.

ÉAMONN CEANNT: THE POPE'S UILLEANN PIPER

DAITHÍ Ó CORRÁIN

É amonn Ceannt (1881–1916) is the least fêted of the seven signatories of the proclamation although he was, as one contemporary put it, 'more naturally a physical force man than any of the other leaders'. He refused to enter the civil service on the basis that it was British and instead secured a clerkship in the city treasurer's office of Dublin Corporation. Like many of his generation, Ceannt was deeply influenced by the arousal of national consciousness occasioned by the centenary of the 1798 Rebellion. The following year, he joined the Gaelic League and began to use the Irish form of his name. He was a dedicated student of the Irish language, a frequent visitor to the Connemara Gaeltacht, taught Irish classes in the early 1900s, and was elected to the *ard choiste* (governing body) of the Gaelic League. Through the Gaelic League, he met Frances ('Áine') O'Brennan, whom he married in an Irish ceremony in June 1905. They had one son named Rónán and Ceannt fought a successful three-year battle to have the birth registered in Irish. This was typical of his resolve and conviction. An accomplished musician, Ceannt developed a keen interest in the uilleann pipes and was honorary secretary of Cumann na bPíobairí Baile Átha Cliath (Dublin Pipers' Club).

Politically, Ceannt was an advanced nationalist. In 1907 he joined the Sinn Féin party, which opposed Home Rule, and he was involved in that body's unsuccessful opposition to the visit of King George V to Ireland in 1911. He was credited with hoisting a banner near Trinity College stating: 'Thou art not conquered yet, dear Land.' That year, Ceannt was sworn into the Irish Republican Brotherhood (IRB) and became a member of its supreme council in 1915. A founder member of the Irish Volunteers, he was involved in financing the procurement of arms and was present at the landing of guns at Howth in July 1914. After the split in the Volunteers, following John Redmond's (1856–1918) pledge of support for the British war effort, Ceannt was elected financial secretary and was also director of communications. Committed to insurrection, along with Pearse and Plunkett, he formed the IRB's military council, which secretly made plans for a Rising. As Commandant 4th Battalion, Dublin Brigade, Ceannt occupied the South Dublin Union during Easter Week. Those under his command recalled his cheerfulness, coolness under fire and bravery. His small force of forty-two fought tenaciously against far superior numbers until Thomas MacDonagh brought news of Pearse's surrender order in person on 30 April. At first, Ceannt was unwilling to give up the fight, but dutifully obeyed the order. He was tried by court martial on 3 and 4 May, found guilty, and executed on 8 May 1916.

Throughout his life, Ceannt displayed an uncompromising devotion to faith and fatherland. Joe Doolan recalled how during Easter Week, Ceannt assembled the garrison each evening to recite the Rosary and prayers. Father Albert Bibby, a Capuchin priest from Church Street Friary, who, with his confrère, Fr Augustine Hayden, accompanied the condemned men to the prison yard and anointed them, told Áine Ceannt of how her husband 'smiling, spoke a few moments before his death of meeting Pope Pius X for whom he played the pipes in Rome'. In September 1908, the Irish Catholic Young Men's Society (CYMS) organised a pilgrimage to mark the sacerdotal jubilee of Pope Pius X. The pilgrims comprised representatives of Dublin Corporation, Dublin confraternities and the CYMS. They left Dublin to the strains of 'God bless the Pope' played by Ceannt – the official piper. To celebrate the pope's jubilee, the International Federation of Catholic Young Men's Societies had organised an international sports meeting at which the Irish team performed admirably. On the team's return to Dublin, the president of the CYMS stated pointedly that they had gone to Rome to testify to their faith *and* fatherland. While their faith was not in any doubt, Ireland's distinct nationality, he suggested, had been almost forgotten on the continent. This, the pilgrims, and Ceannt in particular, sought to rectify. Indeed, the piper determined to speak only Irish while abroad.

On 24 September, Pius X received almost two hundred Irish pilgrims in the consistorial hall. After the pope's address, for the first time in centuries, the skirl of the uilleann pipes was then heard. Attired in a traditional piper's costume, which, according to Áine Ceannt, 'created rather a stir in the streets of Rome' (it is now in the National Museum of Ireland), Ceannt marched the length of the hall playing 'O'Donnell Abú'. When the playing ended, the pope, who took a personal interest in the cultivation of music, directed Ceannt to come forward so that he might inspect the pipes, after which he was asked to play another short air. Appropriately, Ceannt played 'The Wearing of the Green'. In a very simple but powerful way he demonstrated Ireland's distinct national identity. Ceannt's audience with the pope was a remarkable experience. That he recalled it vividly before dying emphasises how dear to his soul were his religion and patriotism. Those same convictions helped ensure that the dead signatories of 1916 underwent a swift and lasting process of secular sanctification.

FURTHER READING

Brian Barton, *From Behind a Closed Door: Secret Court Martial Records of the 1916 Easter Rising* (Belfast: Blackstaff Press, 2002).

Áine Ceannt statement to Bureau of Military History, 27 May 1949, (WS 264), available at Military Archives, Cathal Brugha Barracks, Rathmines, Dublin, www.bureauofmilitaryhistory.ie/reels/bmh/BMH. WS0264.pdf.

Michael Foy and Brian Barton, *The Easter Rising* (Stroud: Sutton Publishing, 1999).

Mary Gallagher, *16 Lives: Éamonn Ceannt* (Dublin: The O'Brien Press, 2014).

William Henry, *Supreme Sacrifice: The Story of Éamonn Ceannt* (Cork : Mercier Press, 2005).

Piaras F. Mac Lochlainn (ed.), *Last Words: Letters and Statements of the Leaders Executed After the Rising at Easter 1916* (Dublin: Kilmainham Jail Restoration Society, 1971).

Charles Townshend, *Easter 1916: The Irish Rebellion* (London: Penguin, 2005).

THOMAS CLARKE: CARDINAL LOGUE, FATHER O'KANE AND THE VOICES OF 1916

RODDY HEGARTY

The collected papers of Cardinal Michael Logue (1840–1924), Archbishop of Armagh from 1887 until his death in 1924, housed in the Cardinal Tomás Ó Fiaich Memorial Library and Archive, are virtually mute with regard to Easter 1916. However, the paucity of the archival record is more than compensated for by a unique collection of recordings made by Fr Louis O'Kane (1906–73), a priest of the Archdiocese of Armagh, in the 1960s and afterwards, including an interview with Kathleen Clarke (1878–1972), the widow of Thomas Clarke (1858–1916).

Cardinal Logue's wide correspondence pays limited attention to the Rising. The events of Easter Week are greatly overshadowed by considerations around the Great War, the relationship with Westminster and the Church's later over-reliance on the abortive Irish Convention – established by Prime Minister David Lloyd George (1863–1945) to discuss self-government for Ireland, the convention sat between July 1917 and April 1918 – to achieve a political resolution to the constitutional question. Logue demonstrated little obvious sympathy for the nationalist cause, unlike his counterpart in Dublin, Archbishop William Walsh (1841–1921). Walsh, it appears, sought the cardinal's support for a church gate collection to alleviate suffering in Dublin following the Rising but this was not taken forward for fear that it would give the impression that the Church was favouring the insurgents. As for the Rising itself, it scarcely raises a mention in Logue's papers. A brief minute of a meeting in Maynooth on 19 June 1916 states that a small group, including the then Bishop of Raphoe, Dr Patrick O'Donnell (1856–1927), was appointed to prepare a statement 'setting forth the Catholic doctrine on Insurrection'. There is some indication that Bishop O'Donnell set to work on this but, as the committee did not meet again until the following October, events had passed the hierarchy by and the statement remained unpublished.

Years later, an altogether more sympathetic interlocutor, Fr Louis O'Kane, set about interviewing veterans of that pivotal period. In 1958, Fr O'Kane had received a tape recorder as a gift; however he did not begin to record veterans of the Irish Volunteers until 1963 when he interviewed south Armagh native, Eddie Boyle. Recognising the benefit of recording these voices, he re-established contact with Seamus Dobbyn, whose father and O'Kane's godfather, Louis Smith, were old Fenians, active in the organisation from the 1860s. Dobbyn, it was claimed, played a central role in Éamon de Valera's escape from Lincoln Prison. One of two books owned by de Valera (1882 –1975), which form part of the library collection, include a biography of Wolfe Tone (1763–98), with the following inscription in Irish: 'This book was given to me on loan in Lincoln Prison, May 1918' – just weeks before the prison break. Following his interaction with Dobbyn, O'Kane began a more systematic effort to record the stories of those that he encountered. Few of his subjects, who were almost exclusively northerners, had contact with the Bureau of Military History and would otherwise have been deprived of the opportunity to recount their experiences. Just as curious is his apparent decision to stop the process in the early 1970s. He may have been influenced by the commencement of the Troubles; he was always conscious that the content of the recordings was delicate, to the extent that they were stored over the border with another priest in County Monaghan.

Among the one hundred and twenty or so recordings is an interview with Kathleen Clarke from 1968. Clarke had lost both her husband Thomas, who was raised in Dungannon, and her brother, Ned Daly, in the executions that followed the Rising. She provides a vivid insight into her husband's attitude towards Roger Casement, in particular, for whom she had little time. Referring to Casement's efforts to raise an Irish Brigade from the ranks of Irish prisoners of war in Germany, she contended that he had 'made a fool of himself' and that the leadership 'didn't ask Germany for men ... All they asked them for was arms'. Clarke further reflects on her husband's motivation and the timing of the Rising while England was at war:

> I couldn't ever see, with the small might that we could throw up against the immense might of the Empire, and he [Tom] said 'but, when they'll be at war, we can have the opportunity of that'. But what he didn't count on was that other forces, supposed to be national, came in and changed the plans in every way.

Thomas Clarke is also represented in the library and archive collection, in the form of a poetic manuscript entitled 'My Jimmy Dear'. Clarke composed the piece in the 1880s and he rediscovered it for Seán MacDiarmada's paper *Irish Freedom* in 1912.

As regards Clarke's spiritual life, there is little to suggest that he was a person of faith in the conventional sense. Although raised in his mother's Catholic faith – his father was a member of the Church of Ireland – he was alienated from the Church because of its position on the Fenians. On the eve of his death, he refused to repudiate his involvement in the Rising when confronted by a would-be confessor: 'I was not sorry for what I had done ... I was not going to face my God with a lie on my tongue.' Other later accounts have him receive the sacraments before he was executed on the morning of 3 May 1916, along with Patrick Pearse and Thomas MacDonagh.

Father O'Kane freely engaged with men and women who had been involved in armed conflict either in 1916 or in the War of Independence, and seems to have done so with little or no judgement on his part. In this way he was able to unearth a rich seam of characters who made up the leadership and ranks of the Volunteers – shopkeepers, farmers, veterans of the Great War, Protestants, Catholics, men and women – all voices of 1916. Seen together, these collections offer a much more rounded sense of the Rising than could ever be garnered from the archives of the primatial see in general or of Cardinal Logue in particular.

FURTHER READING

Helen Litton, *16 Lives: Thomas Clarke* (Dublin: The O'Brien Press, 2014).

Gerard MacAtasney, *Tom Clarke: Life, Liberty, Revolution* (Dublin: Merrion Press, 2012).

CON COLBERT: ASCETIC REVOLUTIONARY

JOSEPH MACMAHON

Con Colbert (1888–1916) supposedly told a fellow prisoner after the failure of the Rising that he expected to be executed and added, 'We are all ready to meet our God', a measure of his confident faith and untroubled conscience. A frequent saying of his was, 'First serve God and then your country'. God, country and family were the loyalties of his short life. His faith in God was simple, trusting and grateful, having been nurtured in a traditional Catholic family environment in west Limerick and reinforced by nationalist circles in Dublin where he joined the Gaelic League and the scouting organisation, Fianna Éireann. Though the national cause absorbed all his attention and energy – he was later recruited to the Irish Republican Brotherhood and served with the Irish Volunteers – his faith was the horizon against which his entire life unfolded.

He accepted that he was an average man endowed with limited ability, and was humble enough to recognise and acknowledge his shortcomings as he struggled against self-serving ambition. What elicited the admiration and affection of those who knew him was his personal integrity and single-minded dedication. He did ordinary things with extraordinary zeal.

Colbert had a strong sense of vocation, of being summoned to serve his country in its hour of need. Did he regard this as a call from God? It would not be surprising if he did, given the almost universal call to his generation throughout Europe to serve God and country. For him, patriotism was a God-given virtue and refusing to live it would be sinful. The summons to serve Ireland was a sacred call that both inspired and demanded a self-sacrificing response. Like many of his comrades, his view of the national struggle was noble, romantic and idealistic. It was not simply about political, economic and cultural freedom, but also involved a moral revolution by saving the soul of Ireland. While it embraced Catholic, Protestant and Dissenter, his vision of the 'new Ireland' was narrow in that there was no place for the Unionist tradition.

In his notion of call and response there are echoes of the gospel beatitude of the pure of heart exhibited in the degree of his unwavering loyalty, uncluttered vision and personal discipline. His time and money were gladly given to the cause but, more tellingly, fully aware that death would almost certainly be the inevitable outcome of his choice, he surrendered his desire for marriage and family, not wishing to bring such sorrow on a future wife and children. The devotional practices of his faith, such as fasting and abstinence (he was also a Pioneer), and his moral rectitude, merged harmoniously with the dedicated commitment to the national movement. Prayer was woven into the ordinary concerns and needs of daily life, as when he would ask a neglected soul in purgatory to awaken him in the morning in return for his fervent prayers. However, he was no gloomy fanatic. His deep faith, expressed spontaneously and publicly, and his conviction of the moral rightness of the cause afforded him an inner freedom that allowed him to be both serious and full of fun and laughter.

His final hours, as described by Sheila Murphy – also a prisoner in Kilmainham – and in the eleven farewell letters he wrote, convey with simplicity something of his spiritual life. His faith was a pervading and consoling bulwark for him in times of personal distress, and it allowed him to resign himself to the inevitability of death, a stance that impressed his dejected companions and lifted their spirits. Looking back, he has no regrets and indeed is grateful for the honour to die for Ireland. He has no fear of dying and is at peace and ready to meet his Creator. He acknowledges his personal sins and also recognises his negligence and want of affection for his family and friends. In these last hours he declines the chance to meet with his nearest because he wants to spare them sorrow and instead asks for their prayers that he will die in God's grace. With confident hope he trusts that they will all meet in heaven 'in happier circumstances' and he looks forward to meeting those who have gone before him. With God's grace he will be able to pray for his family and friends from heaven. In the meantime, he writes to his friends Annie and Lily Cooney: 'May God grant you freedom soon in the fullest sense.' He was executed in Kilmainham Gaol on 8 May 1916.

Colbert's memorial card bears the verse from Horace, *dulce et decorum est pro patria mori* ('it is both sweet and noble to die for one's country'), without any hint of cynicism – what the great anti-war poet Wilfred Owen (1893–1918), in his poem of the same title written in 1917, describes as the 'old Lie'.

FURTHER READING

Seán Brady, 'Some Recollections of 1916 Leaders', *Mungret Annual* (Limerick: Mungret College, 1966), pp. 19–20.

John O'Callaghan, *16 Lives: Con Colbert* (Dublin: The O'Brien Press, 2015).

JAMES CONNOLLY: MINISTRATIONS OF THE CAPUCHIN FRIAR, ALOYSIUS TRAVERS

BRIAN KIRBY

William Patrick Travers was born into a devoutly Catholic family in Cork in 1870. He entered the Capuchin order in 1887, took the name Aloysius and was ordained a priest in 1894. A crusader for temperance and an advocate for the poor and impoverished, he was appointed president of Fr Mathew Hall on Church Street, inaugurating the *Feis Maitiú* in 1909 to promote the Gaelic revival. He was a personal friend of some of the leaders of the nationalist movement, notably Eoin MacNeill (1867–1945), Éamon de Valera and Patrick Pearse, who had argued for closer cooperation between the Gaelic League and Fr Aloysius's temperance movement, 'in the cause that is common to both – the regeneration of Ireland'. In 1916, Fr Aloysius was Provincial Minister of the Irish Capuchins.

During Easter Week 1916, Church Street was the location of some of the bitterest street fighting. Father Mathew Hall became a refuge for local people and many of the Capuchin friars ministered to the wounded, conveying the most serious cases to Richmond Hospital. On Saturday, 29 April, word came that Pearse had ordered a ceasefire. However, the Irish Volunteers on Church Street and North King Street refused to believe it, claiming it was a ruse. On Sunday morning, 30 April, Fr Aloysius, accompanied by his confrère, Fr Augustine Hayden, went to Dublin Castle seeking a permit to see Patrick Pearse who was a prisoner in Arbour Hill. At the castle, the Capuchin friars were allowed to meet with James Connolly (1868–1916): this was the first time Fr Aloysius had encountered the prominent labour leader. Connolly confirmed that the surrender was genuine. At Arbour Hill, the friars obtained from Pearse a signed copy of the surrender order, which they conveyed to Thomas MacDonagh at Jacob's Factory and to Éamonn Ceannt at the South Dublin Union.

On Monday, 1 May, Connolly sent a message to Church Street requesting that Fr Aloysius come to see him. The Capuchin friar left an account of their meeting:

> I returned to the ward or room where Connolly lay. The soldier left and I was alone with Connolly. I told him that I had given my word I would act only as a priest and not in any political capacity. 'I know that, Father,' he said, 'you would not get this privilege otherwise, and it is as a priest I want to see you. I have seen and heard of the brave conduct of the priests and nuns during the week and I believe they are the best friends of the workers.'

On Tuesday, 2 May, Fr Aloysius received a request from Pearse to visit him in Kilmainham Gaol. When he informed Pearse that Connolly had received the sacraments, he responded, 'Thank God. It is the one thing I was anxious about.' It was Fr Aloysius' intention to stay with Pearse until his execution, but he was not permitted to remain; the next day the friar returned to the jail and protested to the authorities. At all the subsequent executions a priest was allowed to remain until the end. On 7 May, Fr Aloysius went to see the Irish

Nationalist MP, John Dillon, in an attempt to bring a halt to the executions. He explained to Dillon 'how the feeling among the working classes in the city was becoming extremely bitter over these executions and this feeling is strong even among those who had no sympathy whatever ... with the Rising'.

However, on the night of Thursday, 11 May, Fr Aloysius received a message from the castle saying his services would be required there at two o'clock in the morning. The Capuchin friar heard James Connolly's last Confession in the hospital in the early hours of 12 May.

> Before leaving for Kilmainham, I had a few words with Connolly. I said that the men who would execute him were soldiers – probably they knew nothing about him, and, like soldiers, would simply obey orders and fire. I wanted him to feel no anger against them, but to say, as Our Blessed Lord said on Calvary, 'Father, forgive them.' 'I do Father,' Connolly answered. 'I respect every man who does his duty.'

Father Aloysius stood behind the firing party as Connolly was placed on a chair and shot. 'It was a scene I should not ask to witness again,' Fr Aloysius later remarked, 'I had got to know Connolly – to wonder at his strength of character ... [and] now I had to say goodbye. All I could do was to return to Church Street and to offer the Holy Sacrifice for his soul. May he rest in peace.'

Father Aloysius remained active on behalf of Dublin's poor for the rest of his life. He was a lifelong friend and admirer of Jim Larkin (1874–1947) who, during his final illness, requested the services of the priest. Father Aloysius administered the last sacraments to him on 24 January 1947 and Larkin died five days later. Thus, Fr Aloysius attended to both of Dublin's most famed labour leaders at their end.

FURTHER READING

Joe Connell, *Rebels' Priests: Ministering to Republicans, 1916–24* (Dublin: Kilmainham Tales, 2014).

Father Aloysius Travers OFM Cap., 'Easter Week 1916: Personal Recollections', *Capuchin Annual* (Dublin: Irish Province of the Capuchin Franciscans, 1942), pp. 211–20.

EDWARD DALY: DAPPER YOUNG MAN

LIAM IRWIN

Edward Daly (1891–1916), one of the youngest of those
executed in the aftermath of the Rising, was a handsome,
dapper, young man. Although he languished for a period in
a series of dull jobs as an accounts clerk, firstly in his native
Limerick and then in Dublin, he remained steadfast in his
ambition to become a soldier. Unlike many of the other 1916
leaders, who left manifestos, letters, poems and other writings,
which provide insights into their character and motivation,
Daly wrote nothing on his political or personal beliefs and
only a handful of his brief letters has survived. These provide
little information about his inner life, and nothing on his
spiritual beliefs. One letter of interest mentions his intention
to marry, a proposal that was otherwise undocumented and
apparently only revealed to one of his sisters. The marriage
did not take place and it is clear from the letter that he was
fearful of his mother's reaction to his plans. He had a very
close relationship with her, always referring to her, even as an
adult, as 'mamma'; his uncle, the Fenian, John Daly (1845–
1916), felt that he had been spoilt by her. This is not unlikely
given that he was born six months after his father's death and
was the longed-for son after eight older sisters.

His initial primary education was by the Presentation
Sisters, who taught boys in their Sexton Street convent
school until the age of seven, and then at the nearby
Christian Brothers. At the age of ten, he made his first Holy

Communion, the normal age at this time, prior to the change introduced in 1910 by Pope Pius X. It is clear that both at home and at school he would have received the normal faith foundation and instruction of the period. However, if his academic record is any guide, he would not have studied Christian doctrine very diligently, as he did not perform well at school and left the CBS at the age of fifteen. After a year taking a commercial course at the secular Leamy's School, he obtained a position as a clerk, initially in Spaight's timber yard and then in his uncle's bakery shop. His main ambition, however, was to be a professional singer – a not unrealistic aim, given his impressive baritone singing voice, but one that he was unable to pursue – or to be a soldier in the British army, an even less practical prospect for someone from his fiercely nationalist family. This was clearly an unhappy period of his life, made worse by a deteriorating relationship with his uncle–employer, which culminated in a final row and his decision to move to Dublin where he lived with his older sister, Kathleen Clarke. Here he became involved in politics, and on their formation in 1913, joined the Irish Volunteers. This was to lead directly to his role in the Rising and sentence of death in its aftermath.

The main sources of any insight into his motivation include an account that his sister Madge later wrote of her and her two sisters' last meeting with their brother shortly before his execution, and the testimony of a priest who was with him later that night. Father Columbus Murphy, one of four Capuchin friars who gave the last rites to the condemned men early in the morning of 4 May, recalled that when he entered Daly's cell he saw 'a look of relief and gladness' on his face. He made his Confession and then received Holy Communion. Again Fr Columbus noted his 'great fervour' as he prepared to die. Another of the Capuchins later wrote, 'I remember well seeing him coming down from the prison cell where he had been to Confession and received Holy Communion. He was calm and brave and ... wished to be remembered to the Sisters of Charity, Brunswick Street, who were known to him and had been very kind.'

Madge Daly's account concentrates on the pride he expressed in his actions during the Rising and the sisters' emotional farewell to him. There is no mention of any religious discussion and no reference to his having any items such as a prayer book or Rosary beads; the items he gave them as mementos – his toothbrush, tobacco pipe, pencil and note case – were all personal, secular objects. He did not write any final letters, merely asking his sisters to convey messages to his mother and other family members. His last recorded words were to say goodbye to the prisoner in the adjoining cell as he walked to face the firing squad. On learning of his death, his mother's reaction was to offer thanks to God for giving her such a brave son.

FURTHER READING

Helen Litton, *16 Lives: Edward Daly* (Dublin: The O'Brien Press, 2013).

Dulce et decorum est pro patria mori.

ı nvíl-cuımne ar

concubar ó colbáırv

a fuaır báſ aſ ſon na
héıſeann

an t-oċtmav lá ve bealtaıne,
1916

Coıſ maſtaſ éıſeann aſ veıſ
vé ʒo ſaıb a anam.

—✠—

PRAY FOR THE SOUL OF

CORNELIUS COLBERT,
Who, with others of his fellow-patriots,
gave his life for Ireland at
Kilmainham Jail

On Monday morning, May 8th, 1916

"Greater love than this no man hath."

PRAYER

BEHOLD, O good and most sweet
Jesus, I cast myself upon my
knees in Thy sight, and with the
most fervent desire of my soul, I pray
and beseech Thee that Thou wouldst
impress upon my heart lively senti-
ments of Faith, Hope and Charity,
with true repentance for my sins
and a firm purpose of amendment,
whilst with deep affection and grief
of soul, I ponder within myself and
mentally contemplate Thy Five most
Precious Wounds, having before my
eyes what the Prophet David put in
Thy mouth concerning Thee, O good
Jesus: "They have dug My hands
and My feet; they have numbered
all My bones."—Ps. xxi, 17, 18.

*A Plenary Indulgence may be gained on
the usual conditions by reciting this prayer
before an image or picture of our Crucified
Redeemer after Confession and Communion,
and praying for the intentions of the Pope.*

GILL   DUBLIN

'Dulce et decorum est pro patria mori' memorial card for Con Colbert
IMAGE COURTESY OF THE IRISH CAPUCHIN PROVINCIAL ARCHIVES

Father Aloysius Travers OFM Cap.

Bedford Row, Limerick, c. 1910. Spaight's timber yard is on the right
IMAGE COURTESY OF THE LIMERICK DIOCESAN ARCHIVE

Limerick troop of Fianna Éireann in front of the Fianna Hall, Barrington Street
IMAGE COURTESY OF THE LIMERICK MUSEUM

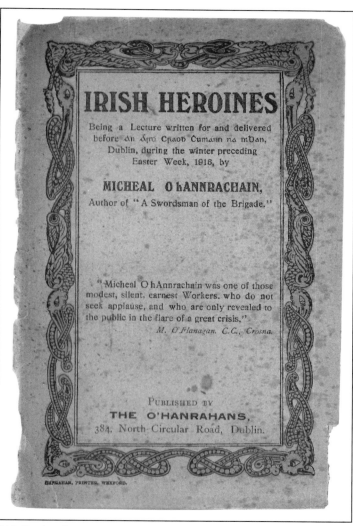

IRISH HEROINES

Being a Lecture written for and delivered
before ᴀn Ꭺ̇ᴘᴅ Cᴘᴀoḃ Cumᴀnn nᴀ mḂᴀn,
Dublin, during the winter preceding
Easter Week, 1916, by

MICHEAL O hANNRACHAIN,

Author of "A Swordsman of the Brigade."

" Micheal O hAnnrachain was one of those
modest, silent, earnest Workers. who do not
seek applause, and who are only revealed to
the public in the flare of a great crisis."

M. O'Flanagan. C.C., Crosna.

PUBLISHED BY
THE O'HANRAHANS,
384, North Circular Road, Dublin.

BANRAHAN, PRINTER, WEXFORD.

Irish Heroines, front cover

49

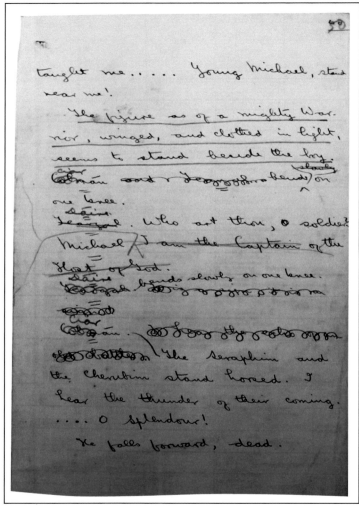

'The figure as of a mighty Warrior', the final page of *The Master*
REPRODUCED BY PERMISSION OF THE LIBRARIAN, MAYNOOTH UNIVERSITY, FROM THE COLLECTIONS OF ST PATRICK'S COLLEGE, MAYNOOTH

said for me loved wife, my life is numbered by
hours now darling. I am drawing nearer and nearer
to god, to that good god who died for us, you and
I love, and our children, and our childrens children,
god and his Blessed mother again and again Bless
and protect you Oh saviour of man if my dear
ones could die and enter heaven with me how Blessed
and happy I would they would be away from the
cares and trials of the world many little one
be a Nun Joseph My little man be a Priest.
if you can James & John to you the care of your
mother make yourselves good strong men for
her sake and Remember Ireland good Bye My Wife
my darling, Remember me, god again bless and
Protect you and our children. I must now Prepare
these last few hours must be spent with god alone
Your loving Husband Michael Mallin
Commandant.
I enclose the buttons off my sleeve   Stephens Green Command
keep them in memory of me
Mike xxxxxx

KMGLM 2012.0054.024

Page 4 of Michael Mallin's last letter to his wife Agnes, written on the eve of his
execution

Altar panel depicting *The Death of St Joseph*, now in the Pearse Museum, Rathfarnham

PHOTOGRAPH BY CAROLINE M. MCGEE WITH THE PERMISSION OF THE PEARSE MUSEUM, ST ENDA'S PARK, RATHFARNHAM

SEÁN HEUSTON: 'PRAY FOR ME. SEAGHÁN MACAODHA'

CATRIONA CROWE

Jesus, Mary, and Joseph, I give you my heart and my soul.
Jesus, Mary, and Joseph, assist me in my last agony.
Jesus, Mary, and Joseph, may I die in peace,
and in your blessed company.

In the hour before his execution, Seán Heuston (1891–1916) found strength in this and other prayers as he knelt in his cold dark cell in Kilmainham Gaol with the Capuchin friar, Fr Albert Bibby, who attended to administer the last rites. On the evening of Sunday, 7 May 1916, Heuston received confirmation that he was to be shot by firing squad in the early hours of Monday morning, as a consequence of his part in the Easter Rising. Father Albert from Church Street Friary arrived at Seán's cell at 3.20 a.m. on Monday and found him holding his Rosary beads and kneeling in prayer in the dim light of a small candle. Thinking of Ireland, his family and friends, Seán, together with Fr Albert, recited acts of faith, hope, love and contrition, as he faced his death at just twenty-five years of age.

Seán Heuston was born at 24 Lower Gloucester Street, Dublin, on 21 February 1891. Christened in St Mary's Pro-Cathedral as John Joseph, he was known to his family and friends as Jack or Seán. His parents John Heuston and Mary Christina McDonald were married in 1888. Between 1889 and 1897 they had four children: Mary, Seán, Teresa and

Michael. The Heustons were a religious family – Seán's sister Mary was a Dominican nun based in Galway in 1916, while his younger brother Michael was a novice in the Dominican Priory in Tallaght. Seán was educated by the Christian Brothers, where he proved to be intelligent and studious in all subjects.

Seán and his siblings grew up in poor circumstances, living in a tenement in Dublin. His sister Teresa suffered from tuberculosis as a child. By the time of the 1901 Census, their father was absent and the family had moved in with their mother's sister, Teresa McDonald. As the eldest boy, it fell to Seán to provide for the family and that, combined with his intellectual abilities, prompted him to apply in 1907 for the much sought-after role of clerk with the Great Southern and Western Railway.

His successful appointment led Seán, at the young age of sixteen, to a posting in Limerick city where he first became involved in nationalist activities. The Wolfe Tone Club was set up in Limerick in 1911 as a facade for the Irish Republican Brotherhood, and Seán was one of its first members. Later that year, Heuston was influential in the establishment and organisation of the Limerick troop of Fianna Éireann, a nationalist scouting organisation for boys aged between eight and eighteen. In late 1913, he returned to Dublin where he joined the Irish Volunteers at its formation, while also rising through the ranks of the Fianna. By 1916, he had become captain of 'D' Company of the 1st Battalion of the Dublin Brigade of the Irish Volunteers.

On Easter Monday, 24 April 1916, a small contingent of thirteen men led by Heuston seized the Mendicity Institution on Dublin's quays on the orders of James Connolly. The strategy was to prevent reinforcements from the Royal Barracks from reaching the Irish Volunteer stronghold, which was being established at the Four Courts. Their orders were to remain at this outpost for just three hours, but by the afternoon the men were under siege from British troops. A small number of reinforcements were sent from the GPO on Tuesday, but eventually around midday on Wednesday, 26 April, surrounded, under grenade attack and having suffered casualties, Heuston agreed to surrender. At his court-martial in Richmond Barracks on Thursday, 4 May, Seán Heuston was sentenced to death for his participation in the Rising.

The following Sunday, prisoners in Kilmainham attended Mass in the chapel but only Seán Heuston and the three other men to be executed early on Monday morning received Holy Communion. His family came to visit him in his cell and he asked many times, in person and in his letters to family, friends and all that knew them, to pray for him after he had gone. He wrote to his sister Mary in Galway asking for her prayers. A short note to his cousin read 'Pray for me. Seaghán MacAodha'. Close to 3.45 a.m. on Monday, 8 May 1916, blindfolded and handcuffed, Seán walked with Fr Albert to the yard in Kilmainham Gaol, repeating the same prayers. His last words as he was shot by firing squad were 'My Jesus, mercy'.

FURTHER READING

Father Albert OFM Cap., 'How Seán Heuston Died: From a Letter by the Late Father Albert OFM Cap.', *Capuchin Annual* (Dublin: Irish Province of the Capuchin Franciscans, 1966), pp. 305–6.

James J. Brennan, 'The Mendicity Institution Area', *Capuchin Annual* (Dublin: Irish Province of the Capuchin Franciscans, 1966), pp. 189–92.

Madge Daly, 'Seán Heuston's Life and Death for Ireland', *Limerick's Fighting Story 1916–21* (Cork: Mercier Press, 2009), pp. 75–80.

John Gibney, *16 Lives: Seán Heuston* (Dublin: The O'Brien Press, 2014).

THOMAS KENT: TOTAL ABSTAINER

GEARÓID BARRY

It was a duty the young curate could hardly have anticipated performing. Father Patrick Sexton, chaplain at the Cork Military Hospital, was used to tending to men off hospital ships from the Great War. Now, on the morning of 9 May 1916, the priest was at the nearby detention barracks – today Cork Prison – ministering to a condemned man. Tried by court-martial and sentenced to death five days earlier on 4 May for 'wilful murder' while participating in armed rebellion, Thomas Kent (1865–1916) entrusted to Fr Sexton one of his prized possessions, requesting that after his death his temperance badge would be given to Fr Michael Ahearne, a priest in his home village of Castlelyons in east Cork: 'From him I got it and I wish it to be returned to him untarnished. He may like to get it. Good-bye.'

Thomas Kent's rebellion has been well summarised in new or reissued publications. If imagined as newsreel, its key scenes might be the dawn firefight at Bawnard House, the Kent family home; Bawnard's first fatality, RIC Head Constable William Rowe who lies dead after the fray; and Tom, arrested afterwards, his hands bound, being marched away in stockinged feet, captured in an iconic photograph. There is a longer story here though, too, that of the Kent family's 'pre-revolution' and their conjugation of patriotism with religion. Not all men and women of 1916 thought exactly like Thomas Kent. For him, civic commitment and religious zeal went hand in hand; his temperance badge is an intriguing point

57

of entry into those sensibilities. Members of the Pioneer and Total Abstinence Association, founded in 1898, took a public pledge to refrain from alcohol for life and were encouraged to pray to the Sacred Heart of Jesus in reparation for the sins drink occasioned. The badge was both an act of faith and of patriotism: 'Ireland sober' would be 'Ireland free'. Like Terence MacSwiney (1879–1920), his kindred spirit from the Gaelic League, Kent was a total abstainer, spurning tobacco also, reputedly refusing the offer of a stimulant on his way to meet the firing squad, and saying: 'I have been a total abstainer all my life and a total abstainer I'll die. I have done my duty as a solider of Ireland and in a few moments I hope to see the face of my God.'

Roy Foster writes that when revolution came, 'the language of religion came naturally to its supporters'. Kent and MacSwiney were thus suited and yet also a contrasting pair. They worked together in Cork in 1915 to re-organise the Irish Volunteers after the split with John Redmond, but whereas MacSwiney grew up in a lower middle-class city family that had seen better times, the Kents were a comfortably-off farming family – their home spacious enough to include, revealingly, an oratory. Both shared a thirst for self-betterment, which had found the perfect outlet in the Irish language movement. Long before, as a nineteen-year-old emigrant in Boston, in his spare time from work in a Catholic publishing house, Kent had helped to found the Philo-Celtic Society. The founding impulse of this Cumann Carad na Gaeilge or 'society of friends of the Irish language' was to promote Irish cultural modes amongst the immigrant Irish of the east-coast United States.

Clergy and religious, sometimes related, feature repeatedly in the Kents' lives. Their mother had two brothers who were priests in their home diocese of Cloyne. In 1889, shortly before Thomas' return home, the Kent brothers teamed up with local curate, Fr Jeremiah O'Dwyer, to respond to the eviction of their Rice cousins. Four of the brothers, and Fr O'Dwyer himself, were among a group of ten defendants at a subsequent sensational trial at Fermoy for instigating a boycott and evading payment of rents. Convictions and stiff punishment from the bench followed for most of the defendants, including the priest. Back in Castlelyons, Thomas was part of a generation of men and women that threw themselves into cultural nationalism with gusto, from the GAA to Irish dancing to Gaelic League dramas, the latter inspired in part by local parish priest and noted Gaelic author Peadar Canon Ó Laoghaire. 'An tAthair Peadar' was one of the first on the scene at Bawnard the morning of the family's arrest and his remains lie in the same churchyard as those of the Kent brothers.

In the spirit of the times, MacSwiney's and Kent's was a muscular Christianity. They were tried together but acquitted of making seditious speeches against recruitment in early 1916. Kent enlisted the famed Dungourney hurling team to disrupt a recruitment meeting. 'Sacrifice' was no mere abstraction for the Kent family, however. The widow Mary Kent, mother to nine children, had endured seeing most of her seven sons, her fourth son Tom included, doing penal servitude for organising non-payment of rent during the prolonged Land War between 1881 and 1903. In the space of a fateful week in May 1916, this remarkable matriarch was buffeted by the death of two sons – Thomas and Richard, her youngest – whilst another, David, was interned. She died in January 1917. However, she was not the only woman who mourned after Bawnard. Constable Rowe's widow, Sarah Jane Splaine, faced the unenviable task of raising five children, aged between eight and thirteen, on a less than generous settlement from her husband's state employers.

Ninety-nine years later, the elegiac and dignified state funeral of 'forgotten Volunteer' Thomas Kent at Castlelyons on 17 September 2015 held the nobility and human tragedy of 1916 in equipoise. At the requiem Mass, homilist Bishop William Crean of Cloyne acknowledged war's cruelty and that 'a certain tentative mood prevails in our time, uncertain of the worth of violent resistance'. Zeal for justice, properly understood, was the mark of Thomas Kent, however, 'one such man amongst others, women and men who shared his dream ... the dream of freedom'. The grammar of Irish identity has largely shifted from religion and nationalism to a civic one in the interim, but that essential point endures. The bishop's calm appreciation of Kent's sacrifice, whilst acknowledging with generosity the messiness of history, might serve us well as an example as we mark this centenary milestone in the life of our country.

FURTHER READING

R. F. Foster, *Vivid Faces: The Revolutionary Generation in Ireland, 1890–1923* (London: Allen Lane, 2014).

Piaras F. MacLochlainn (ed.), *Last Words: Letters and Statements of the Leaders Executed After the Rising at Easter 1916* (Dublin: The Stationery Office, 1990), pp. 155–7.

JOHN MACBRIDE: A VIOLENT VOCATION

GERARD MCNAMEE

Early in the morning of 5 May 1916, a middle-aged man stood stiffly in the dim light of Kilmainham courtyard facing the rifles of a British firing squad. It was an abrupt and violent end to a remarkable life. From the cloistered seclusion of a boarder's life in St Malachy's College, Belfast, to the fiery turmoil of Easter Week in Dublin, the life of John MacBride (1868–1916) was a tale of adventure and controversy.

Among the leaders of the Rising, he has never enjoyed the same level of adulation in the nationalist hagiography, as for example, Pearse or Plunkett. A pragmatic military man, MacBride did not appear to embrace the mystic Catholicism or romantic notions of other leaders. Moreover, his alleged marital misconduct, drunkenness and impetuous nature did not sit well with the aura of martyrdom. Recently, Anthony Jordan and others have done much to give this brave, battle-hardened warrior his rightful place in the pantheon. His exploits in America and South Africa have been well documented. Little is known, however, about his formative years, so perhaps a brief investigation of John MacBride's secondary education may prove instructive.

John was born in Westport Quay, County Mayo, on 8 May 1868, the youngest of five boys. His father was Patrick MacBride from Antrim and his mother, Honoria Gill, was from nearby Clare Island. Patrick, a former ship's captain, ran a pub and grocery business. Having completed their primary education with the Christian Brothers in Westport, the brothers Anthony and John were sent to boarding school in Belfast in 1881. It seems odd that they should be sent so far from home, but the school had strong links with the parishes of the Glens and their father had grown up in Glenshesk.

Then, as now, St Malachy's College was one of Ireland's most prestigious schools. Even though it had already existed for half a century, an impressive building programme had just been completed with a new study hall, chapel, laboratories and library. Set on a hill overlooking Belfast Lough, it was the first school to take advantage of a new system whereby students were permitted to study for degrees conferred by the newly established Royal University of Ireland. Moreover, the college had its own farm, which generated income, so fees were kept at a moderate level. The president at the time, Dr Henry Henry, was one of the most influential churchmen of his day and later became bishop of the diocese.

Boarding fees were received on behalf of the two brothers of £39 in December 1881 and again £30 in June 1882. In 1884, fees are received on behalf of Anthony but there is no mention of John. In 1886, John is back on the roll. In the intervening period he worked as an apprentice to a draper in Castlerea but after two years returned to the college. It was during his time at Castlerea that he first became involved with activists of the Irish Republican Brotherhood (IRB). There was no shortage of like-minded young men in the St Malachy's of the 1880s. In the same class was Eoin MacNeill, later co-founder of the Gaelic League and Commander of the Irish Volunteers. While contemporaries like Jeremiah McVeagh (1870–1932), Thomas Harbison (1864–1930) and T. J. Campbell (1871–1946) would become prominent in nationalist politics, there were some IRB radicals in the making like Patrick McCartan and a few years later Sean McEntee and Joseph Connolly. A remarkable efflorescence of talent marked that decade. Standards were high. Some students would later achieve distinction as leading surgeons, judges and theologians. Anthony MacBride would make his mark in medicine and politics. But when his younger brother left to work in Hugh Moore's pharmacy in Dublin it was just a prelude to military life, both in the Transvaal in South Africa – where he fought alongside the Boers with the Irish Brigade between 1899 and 1900 in the war with Britain – and his later involvement in the Rising.

As regards the curriculum, John MacBride would have studied Latin, Greek, French, Mathematics and Natural Philosophy but no Irish. It would be 1900 before Gearóid Ó Nualláin would return to establish a noble tradition of the language at St Malachy's. His teachers would have included William Firth, the renowned Cambridge mathematician who invented a type of 'magic square', and Dr Thomas Fitzpatrick, author and historian. The main games were rugby and handball. Gaelic football was not played as yet, even though John McKay, the Belfast journalist, had just left the college and would shortly become first secretary of the GAA.

Saint Malachy's College, or 'Vicinage' in those days, was above all a powerhouse of Catholic faith. A monastic routine of prayer and daily Mass was at the core of student life. Perhaps more than any Irish college it produced scores of missionary, religious and diocesan priests. As Major John MacBride walked to his death on that May morning, perhaps the knowledge of the prayers of former colleagues sustained him.

SEÁN MACDIARMADA: FIRM FRIEND, MONSIGNOR PATRICK BROWNE

NOELLE DOWLING

' I , Seán MacDiarmada, before paying the penalty of death for my love of Ireland, and abhorrence of her slavery, desire to make known to all my fellow-countrymen that I die, as I have lived, bearing no malice to any man, and in perfect peace with Almighty God.'

Seán MacDiarmada (1883–1916) was born on a small farm in Kiltyclogher, County Leitrim, on 27 January 1883. It might be assumed that he was a child of his time, brought up in a family that believed in the teachings of the Catholic Church, but there is no evidence to suggest that he was a deeply religious man. His one true passion was the cause of Irish freedom to which he devoted his life, joining the Irish Republican Brotherhood (IRB) in 1906. From the outset, he was actively involved with the Irish Volunteers and travelled throughout the country helping to set up Volunteer clubs. Despite his physical disability – he had contracted polio in 1911 – he was a man of action and very highly regarded by all who worked with him. He has been described as the 'mind of the revolution' and was always trying to find ways of furthering the ideal of Irish independence.

During the course of Easter Week, MacDiarmada was assigned to the GPO where he demonstrated great concern for those around him, as illustrated by his solicitude for the injured when he organised their removal to Jervis Street Hospital. On the first day of the Rising, Monsignor Michael

Curran, who was Secretary to the Archbishop of Dublin, William Walsh, anxious to provide for the spiritual care of the insurgents, arranged that priests from the Pro-Cathedral would hear the Confessions of those garrisoned in the GPO. If MacDiarmada did not avail of the opportunity in the GPO, he did receive the last sacraments in Kilmainham Gaol from the chaplain, Fr Eugene McCarthy. Father McCarthy, who was based in the nearby St James' Church, attended to many of the fourteen leaders who were executed in the jail. On Saturday afternoon, 29 April, MacDiarmada read Pearse's surrender to the surviving members of the garrison who had retreated to Moore Street. He added that their duty was to survive the rebellion and ultimately achieve freedom for Ireland.

MacDiarmada was a very good friend of Monsignor Patrick Browne (1889–1960), a priest of the Dublin Diocese and Professor of Mathematics at St Patrick's College, Maynooth (and later President of University College Galway). Browne visited MacDiarmada twice in the days leading up to his execution, spending five or six hours with him overnight on 10 and 11 May, due to an apparent oversight on the part of the authorities in Kilmainham. MacDiarmada told him that he had made his peace with God. However, his relationship with the Catholic Church was not an easy one. He felt very bitter towards the Church, especially in relation to its treatment of the Fenians, recounting the events surrounding the death and burial of Charles Kickham (1828–82). The local clergy in Thurles had refused to receive his body into the church and none of them attended the burial to recite prayers. MacDiarmada freely admitted to his friend that he had been away from the Church for some time, and yet the language in both his final statement and his last letter to his family contain many references to God and heaven. 'By the time this reaches you I will, with God's mercy, have joined in Heaven my poor father and mother, as well as my dear friends who have been shot during the week. They died like heroes, and with God's help I will act throughout as heroic as they did.'

MacDiarmada was very comfortable in Browne's company, and during their final hours together they recalled their many meetings: in Maynooth, where they played bridge; in a pub on Dublin's Duke Street, The Bailey; or in the offices of the IRB newspaper, *Irish Freedom*. In fact, they had only met about two weeks before the Rising and MacDiarmada was quite surprised that Browne had not picked up on the hints given regarding Easter Week. Friends were very important to MacDiarmada and during his conversation with the monsignor he expressed his concern for Mary Kate ('Kit') Ryan whose arrest, according to Browne, greatly troubled him. Kit was the sister of Josephine Mary ('Min'), MacDiarmada's 'sentimental attachment' – the woman 'who would have been my wife', as he describes her in one of his last letters.

Seán MacDiarmada, together with Connolly, was the last of the leaders to be executed in Kilmainham on 12 May 1916. He had few possessions but his will stipulated that some money be set aside for the celebration of Masses. Following his death, his Rosary beads were given to Monsignor Browne, who paid tribute to his friend in verse shortly after his execution: 'Your pale dead face with sure insistent claim/shall haunt my soul as long as thought endures/waking remembrance of your wasted frame/a fire with that all conquering soul of yours.'

FURTHER READING

Monsignor Patrick Browne statement to Bureau of Military History, 20 October 1952 (WS 729), available at Military Archives, Cathal Brugha Barracks, Rathmines, Dublin, www.bureauofmilitaryhistory.ie/reels/bmh/BMH.WS0729.pdf.

Gerard MacAtasney, *Seán MacDiarmada: The Mind of the Revolution* (Dublin: Drumlin Publications, 2004).

Piaras F. Mac Lochlainn (ed.), *Last Words: Letters and Statements of the Leaders Executed after the Rising at Easter 1916* (Dublin: Kilmainham Jail Restoration Society, 1971).

THOMAS MACDONAGH: 'MAKING ME DARKLY GROPE TO MY SURE END'

SALVADOR RYAN

Thomas MacDonagh (1878–1916) was born in Cloughjordan, County Tipperary, on 1 February 1878 to Joseph and Mary MacDonagh (née Parker), who was a convert from Unitarianism. Both were national school teachers. His mother's adoption of Roman Catholicism heavily influenced the short stories, poems and devotional pieces that she subsequently composed, works which included a treatise in ten chapters entitled 'The Daily Life of a True Catholic – by a Convert', and undoubtedly left their mark on the young Thomas. This was a household in which there was not just the recitation of the family Rosary, but also the reading of advanced spiritual works such as Thomas à Kempis' *The Imitation of Christ*. It was very much a lived faith: for instance, Thomas' mother encouraged her children to recite a litany 'for the relief of the souls in Purgatory' if they could not sleep at night. When it came to the time for secondary education, Thomas was sent to the Holy Ghost Fathers at Rockwell College, outside Cashel, in 1892. This experience, too, would leave a deep impression on him.

By 1894, Thomas had decided he wanted to be a Holy Ghost missionary and, so, entered the junior scholasticate at Rockwell as a first step on the road to priesthood, a move which would see him don a soutane and help out with the instruction of younger students. At the time he declared that, 'It has always been my wish to become a priest and now that wish is stronger than ever'. During this period he would write some devotional poetry of which the following lines are typical: 'O Holy Ghost!/Thou art our comfort in the fight/against the impious world/come down in tongues of heavenly light/dovelike – with wings unfurled.'

But, over time, his youthful religious zeal began to wane, and by 1901 he declared that he had 'no vocation to religious life' and subsequently left Rockwell. In the years leading up to his departure, MacDonagh had experienced periods of intense doubt and, indeed, something approaching despair, especially in the aftermath of the death of a young school-friend and fellow scholastic from whom he had become estranged and never had the opportunity to reconcile. Poem 25, entitled 'Through the Night', from his first collection of poetry, *Through the Ivory Gate* (1903), dates from this period:

> Man comes and lives and goes/Brief honoured and frail .../And when he's had his day/Dies – for all time – who knows?' In the same poem he laments: 'Once – oh how far it seems!/ I could believe at will;/Till came the blighted chill/of dark despairing dreams/which have destroyed my life/making me darkly grope/to my sure end, no hope/for a less bitter strife.

And yet, in poem 31, entitled 'Resurgam', he grasps at the promise of resurrection: 'I trust the Lord that He will raise me up/when silent I have waited in the grave for lonely years.' In the introduction to this collection, MacDonagh explained that his poetry constituted a 'struggle of soul from the innocence of Childhood through disillusion, disappointment and ill doubt; and thence through prayer and hope and the pathos of old memories to lasting Trust and Faith'.

By the time MacDonagh married his Protestant bride, Muriel Gifford, on 3 January 1912, his soul-searching had led him to largely forsake the religious practice of his youth. He wrote to his friend, Dominick Hackett: '... of late the Church here is absurd about mixed marriages. Muriel and I are of the same religion, which is neither Catholic nor Protestant, nor any other form of dogmatic creed; neither of us ever go to church or chapel, but for the sake of several things and people we are willing to conform for a marriage ceremony.'

One of those 'people' may have been his sister, Mary, whose name in religion was Sister Francesca. However, MacDonagh's depiction of nuns at prayer in his poem 'A Dream of Being' also suggests some disillusionment with their particular calling: 'I heard their voices rise and fall and rise/in their long prayer like quiet faded sighs/calling from hearts that lost/their passion long ago.' As it happened, before MacDonagh was executed, his sister Mary did manage to get to see him (when Muriel did not) and she flung a set of Rosary beads around his neck. According to the July 1916 issue of the *Catholic Bulletin*, before his execution, MacDonagh 'knelt for a long time in prayer, on the bare floor of his cell, with his crucifix clasped in his hands'.

An article on Thomas MacDonagh by Rev. A. Raybould in *The Irish Monthly* in September 1919 played down his struggles with faith: 'It has been hinted that Thomas MacDonagh fell away from his childhood's – the Catholic – faith, but surely his poems refute this accusation.' Raybould preferred to regard him as intensely speculative:

'and to the naturally speculative, the practical acceptance of revealed religion must open up a labyrinth of intellectual difficulties; but a thousand difficulties do not make one doubt.' However, such papering over the fissures that often accompany faith does little justice to its lived experience. Many people today who struggle with issues of belief are likely to find MacDonagh's own words in the poem 'The Tree of Knowledge' far more authentic. In presenting a dusky scene in which he sees a 'chalice of sacred gold/filled to the brim with wine', MacDonagh continues: 'I tremble and lie still/Held by a holy dread/Lest the wine from the chalice spill/and the knowledge of God lie dead/I lose the chalice from view/Through infirmity of will.'

FURTHER READING

Shane Kenna, *16 Lives: Thomas MacDonagh* (Dublin: The O'Brien Press, 2015).

Johann A. Norstedt, *Thomas MacDonagh: A Critical Biography* (Charlottesville: University of Virginia Press, 1980).

A. Raybould, 'Thomas MacDonagh', *The Irish Monthly*, xxxvii, no. 555 (September, 1919), pp. 475–9.

MICHAEL MALLIN: THE END OF ALL THINGS EARTHLY

DAMIEN BURKE

Michael Mallin (1874–1916) was shot by firing squad in Kilmainham Gaol on 8 May 1916. Chief of Staff and second-in-command to James Connolly in the Irish Citizen Army, he was leader of the garrison in St Stephen's Green and the College of Surgeons during Easter 1916. His last letter to his wife Agnes, written on the eve of his execution – page four of which is reproduced on page 51 courtesy of Kilmainham Gaol Museum – is a reminder in today's fluid, social-media driven world of the power of the handwritten word (*reproduced as in original*):

> My darling Wife Pulse of my heart, this is the end of all things earthly; sentense of Death has been passed, and a quarter to four tomorrow the sentense will be carried out by shooting and so must Irishmen pay for trying to make Ireland a free nation, Gods will be done.

It is not a calm and collected document. Littered with repetition and punctuation errors, issues such as faith and forgiveness, Ireland's destiny, legacy, love and regret are jumbled up in four short pages. Mallin is beset by emotional turmoil as he begins to comprehend the consequences of his death for his pregnant wife and four young children:

> My heart strings are torne to pieces when I think of you and them of our manly James, happy go lucky John Shy warm Una dadys Girl and oh little Joseph my little man my little man Wife dear Wife I cannot keep the tears back when I think of him he will rest in my arms no more, to think I have to leave you to battle through the world with them without my help, what will you do my own darling ...

At three intervals in the letter, Mallin expresses a wish that he, his wife and children 'could all reach Heaven together', however, he notes, 'that is sinful'. He asks for 'a special favour' of his wife: 'don't give your love to any other man ... perhaps it is selfish of me to ask' but he leaves her 'absolutely free in the matter'. His wish is that Agnes will 'dedicate Una to the service of God and also Joseph, so that we may have two to rest on as penance for our sins'. Una did become a Loreto nun and two sons, John and Joseph, became Jesuits. Whatever regret and responsibility Mallin felt at his impending death, he does not believe that their blood has been shed in vain. 'I believe Ireland will come out greater and grander but she must not forgot she is Catholic she must keep her Faith.'

What inspired Mallin 'to make Ireland a free nation'? Born in a tenement in the Liberties area of Dublin in 1874, he joined the British Army aged fourteen as a drummer boy. While serving in India as part of the Tirah Campaign (1897–9), Mallin experienced an epiphany. He became sympathetic to the Indian struggle for independence and disillusioned with military life. He began to believe that physical force was necessary in removing British rule from Ireland. Discharged in 1902, Mallin subsequently married Agnes Hickey in Dublin. It was while working as a silk weaver in the city in 1908 that Mallin became involved in the trade union movement and was appointed Chief of Staff of the Irish Citizen Army by James Connolly in 1914. In preparation for the Rising, he used his military experience to organise, train and equip the Citizen Army. On 24 April 1916, Mallin occupied St Stephen's Green, appointing Constance Markievicz (1868–1927) as his second-in-command. Question marks remain over Mallin's military leadership, in particular the decision to occupy a park overlooked by tall buildings, which was compounded by the failure to seize the strategic Shelbourne Hotel, further weakening the defence of St Stephen's Green. However, by the time Mallin surrendered on 30 April 1916, he had gained the admiration of those under his command for his bravery and kindness during the Rising.

Michael Mallin was a man of enduring faith. 'So happy and contented' after receiving absolution, he requests prayers 'for my Poor Soul'. He asks forgiveness from Agnes for his 'many transgressions'. 'You have been a true loving wife too good for me ... think only of the happy times we spent together forgive and forget all else.' He is without rancour at the end. 'I find no fault with the soldiers or Police I forgive them from the Bottom of my heart, pray for all the souls who fell in the fight Irish & English.' He briefly alludes to his future remembrance 'tell him (William Partridge who fought with Mallin) I met my fate like a man'. Controversially, at Mallin's court-martial, he denied holding a commission in the Irish Citizen Army and named Constance Markievicz as the senior officer. Perhaps behind this falsehood lies Mallin's wish to live for his wife and children. Conflicted and torn, he was driven by devotion to revolution, on the one hand, and love for his family, on the other. Tragically, in making 'Ireland always come first', he deprived his wife of a husband and his children of a father.

FURTHER READING

Brian Hughes, *16 Lives: Michael Mallin* (Dublin: The O'Brien Press, 2012).

MICHAEL O'HANRAHAN: HEROES AND SAINTS ON THE RED ROAD

BERNIE DEASY and CONN Ó MAOLDHOMHNAIGH

Michael O'Hanrahan (1877–1916) was born in New Ross, County Wexford, the son of Richard O'Hanrahan, a cork cutter, and his wife, Mary Williams. The family resided in Carlow for a time before moving to Dublin around 1902 where O'Hanrahan was associated with various nationalist-leaning organisations. By 1916, he was in the full-time employ of the Irish Volunteers at its headquarters at 2 Dawson Street, Dublin. O'Hanrahan was a member of the 2nd Battalion of the Irish Volunteers, led by his friend, Thomas MacDonagh, which occupied Jacob's Factory during the Easter Rising.

O'Hanrahan was also an author and freelance journalist. Two novels of historical fiction were published in 1914 and 1918, and he wrote for several nationalist newspapers under different pseudonyms. O'Hanrahan's personal papers were seized by the British Army after the Rising, so there is a paucity of sources on which to base discussion of his religious faith. However, there are some useful references in several newspaper articles and his lecture, *Irish Heroines*, delivered to the *ard craobh* (central branch) of Cumann na mBan during the winter of 1915–6, and published in 1917.

Essentially, *Irish Heroines* is a rallying call to the members of Cumann na mBan to be heroic and active in the struggle for Irish freedom. While the lecture is predominately political, O'Hanrahan's exhortations are imbued with religious motifs and imagery that subtended his own spirituality. O'Hanrahan equates heroism with saintliness. Saints are presented as models for living – for O'Hanrahan those who are active in the struggle for Irish freedom are heroes, and 'heroism is just like saintliness'. O'Hanrahan alludes to the saints in their midst, and the failure of the Church and contemporary society to recognise them as such:

> We do not know our saints till they have gone from amongst us ... They perform the many little duties which men and women are called on to perform, with a due respect to the laws of God and man. They perform virtuous actions, do good to their fellow-beings, retire, many of them, far from the haunts of men ... They die. But does the Church recognise them as saints? Does it crown them with the crown of saintliness immediately the grave closes over their heads. No, it does not.

Likewise, 'We do not know our heroes or heroines. They may walk hand in hand with us, but we are blind ... Fortunate indeed is the hero who is known to his generation.' Like saints, heroes have duties to accomplish and they are 'are only performed in times of national crisis or danger'. Moreover, 'the true hero regards his heroic deeds as but duties well performed, and not of particular merit'. The hero is 'seldom gifted with a brazen tongue which, like the Pharisee of old, proclaims his virtues aloud to a blind world ...' Thus, humility and self-abnegation, qualities associated with saints, are also found in heroes. There are autobiographical echoes at play here – O'Hanrahan is variously described by those who knew him as 'a rather quiet retiring man' and 'gentle, quiet and unassuming', and he operated covertly in his work for the Irish Volunteers.

O'Hanrahan also writes that those who do their duty well for the fatherland's welfare have been touched by the 'divine spark'. It is implied that those who are active in the struggle for Irish freedom are doing God's will. This is redolent of statements attributed by the historian Francis P. Jones to O'Hanrahan during his final hours: 'I am ready to give my life for God and my country. In a few hours I shall be with my God, where I will plead the cause of beloved Ireland ... this is God's will, and it is for Ireland.' O'Hanrahan ends *Irish Heroines*, reprising the words of St Paul. Following the achievement of Irish freedom, heroes and heroines 'can whisper in [their] hearts we "fought the good fight; we kept the faith"'.

Under the pseudonym 'Art', O'Hanrahan wrote an article in *Irish Freedom* about the Fianna in November 1910. His use of religious vocabulary continues here. Thus, Robert Emmet's (1778–1803) blood 'consecrated' the gibbet on which he died. O'Hanrahan counsels that Irish freedom can only be won by 'the red road of war'. Interestingly, for one who made part of his living from writing, O'Hanrahan advises that 'The editorial, the article, or the speech, however eloquent, which does not point out that road is so much cant which further enslaves an enslaved people ...' O'Hanrahan further writes that the brand of freedom for which Ireland strives is 'the brand for which Tone's throat was mangled by the British Government in the hope of making it repulsive and its exponent anathema to a deeply religious people such as the Irish'. Michael O'Hanrahan sacrificed his life for his involvement in the Easter Rising, the 'red road' that led to his death sentence and execution at Kilmainham Gaol on 4 May 1916.

FURTHER READING

Conor Kostick, *16 Lives: Michael O'Hanrahan* (Dublin: The O'Brien Press, 2015).

Michael O'Hanrahan, *Irish Heroines* (Dublin: O'Hanrahans, 1917).

PATRICK PEARSE: THE MASTER

BARBARA MCCORMACK

A stranger to the Russell Library at Maynooth University might be surprised to find among the revered medieval manuscripts and early printed books that constitute the historical collections of St Patrick's College, Maynooth, a small innocuous copybook. The copy contains an early draft of *The Master*, a play penned by Irish revolutionary, P. H. Pearse (1879–1916). Written in 1915, the work provides an invaluable insight into his religious and political beliefs.

Although Pearse was born at the height of agrarian conflict in Ireland – the Irish National Land League was founded in October 1879, just three weeks before his birth – he enjoyed a somewhat prosperous upbringing as the son of a successful stonemason and sculptor. He attended a private school and later the CBS on Westland Row, Dublin, before undertaking a degree with the Royal University of Ireland and law courses at Trinity College and King's Inns. Pearse wrote many literary works in Irish and English during his lifetime, including several plays, short stories and poems, but perhaps his greatest work is *The Master*.

According to historian and author Sean Farrell Moran, the play embodies notions of sacrifice and redemption while advocating the use of violence to achieve 'not only national victory but also individual deliverance'. *The Master* was written at a time when Home Rule was no longer a viable option for Pearse and he began to embrace the idea of armed rebellion as a means to an Irish Republic. By 1913, Pearse had started to forge links with the Irish Republican Brotherhood (IRB), eventually becoming a member in December of that year. By the time *The Master* was staged at the Irish Theatre, Hardwick Street, in May 1915, Pearse had already assumed a pivotal role in military operations with the IRB.

The play is set in a small Irish monastery in a secluded woodland in which the main protagonist Ciarán, the master of the title, gives lessons to a small group of boys: Art, Breasal, Maine, Rónán, Ceallach and Iollann Beag. Pearse changed the principal character's name from Colmán during revisions of the text; indeed the manuscript in the Russell Library is littered with annotations and corrections. Externally Ciarán lives a devout life, spending his days praying, fasting and teaching, yet he is plagued with internal doubt. The youngest student, Iollann Beag, on the other hand represents unwavering faith, innocence and devotion. The little monastic school is steeped in faith: Iollann sings about the friendship between Jesus and John the Baptist; Ciarán contemplates the 'scattering' of the twelve apostles; Breasal recites a poem about Mary Magdalene.

Ciarán's seven-year-long peaceful existence in the wilderness is threatened by the arrival of King Dáire and his horsemen, in response to suspicions from the local druids about Ciarán's alleged disregard for ancient customs. Faced with the imminent arrival of Dáire, Ciarán suffers a crisis of faith, exclaiming: 'This seems to me the hardest thing I have tried to do. Can a soldier fight for a cause of which he is not sure? Can a teacher die for a [faith] thing he does not [hold] believe? ... Forgive me, Lord!'

Yet Ciarán refuses to flee, against the wishes of his students Ceallach and Breasal, instead proclaiming: 'He is a sorry champion who forsakes his place of battle. This is my place of battle. You would not have me do a coward thing?'

When Dáire confronts Ciarán – they were boyhood rivals, each competing for glory and recognition – we learn that a life of sacrifice and suffering is worthless without faith. Dáire exclaims: 'Men die for false things, for ridiculous things, for evil things. What vile cause has not its heroes?' Ciarán refuses to fight against the king and yet his sacrifice is meaningless because his faith is weak. Iollann's strength, devotion, and faith is a counterpoise to Ciarán's weakness, pride and lack of faith. When faced with Dáire's sword, Iollann calls on St Michael who appears as 'a mighty Warrior, winged, and clothed in light', and seems to stand beside the boy. Upon witnessing this miracle Ciarán, overcome with emotion, falls down dead.

Faith is central to the play. Ciarán notes that 'faith comes to the humble only' and it is his lack of faith that is ultimately his downfall. Iollann's unwavering devotion, on the other hand, leads to salvation. Within twelve months of the 1915 production of the play, Pearse was dead – as was his brother Willie who played the part of Ciarán in that production. The brothers were executed on 3 and 4 May 1916 respectively, for their part in the Rising. *The Master* provides a fascinating window into the mind of Patrick Pearse, his political but also his religious worldview, in the months leading up to Easter Week.

FURTHER READING

J. J. Lee, 'Pearse, Patrick Henry', *Dictionary of Irish Biography* (Cambridge: Cambridge University Press, 2009).

Sean Farrell Moran, *Patrick Pearse and the Politics of Redemption: The Mind of the Easter Rising, 1916* (Washington DC: Catholic University of America Press, 1997).

Róisín Ní Ghairbhí, *16 Lives: Willie Pearse* (Dublin: The O'Brien Press, 2015).

WILLIAM PEARSE:
A SPIRITUAL THING

CAROLINE MCGEE

On 10 February 1916, Patrick Pearse delivered a Gaelic League lecture on the theme of nationality to a large audience in Waterford. Quoting from his essay 'Ghosts' he said: 'They have conceived of nationality as though it were a material thing, whereas it is a spiritual thing.' Nowhere does the impact of Patrick Pearse's philosophical view have more poignancy than the fate that befell his younger brother William Pearse (1881–1916), the artist-turned-revolutionary who was executed in Kilmainham Gaol, on 4 May 1916 for his part in the Easter Rising.

'Willie' (as he was known) was born on 15 November 1881 at 27 Great Brunswick Street (now Pearse Street) to London-born James Pearse and his second wife Margaret (née Brady). He was initially educated at home but from 1891 attended the Christian Brothers School on Westland Row. In 1897, Willie commenced night classes at the Dublin Metropolitan School of Art (DMSA) while also learning the craft of architectural stone-carving from his father, a journeyman craftsman who migrated to Ireland during the 1850s as the church furnishing market was developing. James Pearse ran a thriving business that had, by the turn of the century, supplied 1,500 altars alone to churches at home and abroad. He died suddenly in 1900 and although Willie was only eighteen he joined his half-brother James Vincent in Pearse and Sons (as it was now called) working on ecclesiastical sculptural commissions for churches in Dublin, Limerick, Mayo, Sligo and Wexford. He continued taking classes at the DMSA and made several trips to Paris, on one occasion visiting the studio of sculptor Auguste Rodin (1840–1917). He also visited many of the city's churches – described by his brother Patrick as 'limewhite palaces [filled with] surging hosts'. The spiritual and aesthetic beauty of these buildings and their contents cannot have failed to impress Willie who very much wanted to have a career as an artist and later described himself as a 'sculptor master'.

Noteworthy commissions executed by Pearse and Sons up to 1910 (when the firm closed) are not just reflective of the extent and reach of the contemporary Irish art industry, which saw church decorating firms achieve success at home and abroad, they are also directly linked to Willie Pearse. The first commision, in 1907, was for an altar in the Sacred Heart Chapel of the Church of St Mary of the Angels, Church Street, Dublin, mother church to the Capuchin friars who administered the last rites to Willie, Patrick and many of the fourteen other men executed for their part in the Easter Rising (the altar was later sold to St Patrick's Church, Drumalee, County Cavan). The next commission was for an altar depicting *The Death of St Joseph* for the Cross and Passion Convent, Bradford, England (1909), while the final work was a statue of the *Mater Dolorosa* (Our Lady of Sorrows) for St Andrew's Church, Westland Row, Dublin, where Willie was Confirmed while a student at the adjacent Christian Brothers school. Contemporary criticism of his work was very positive, the statue of Our Lady being described by cultural nationalist Edward Martyn as 'expressive'. The Bradford altar front (now in the Pearse Museum, Rathfarnham) is also very accomplished, suggesting Willie could have looked forward to a career as a sculptor had the events of Easter 1916 not intervened.

All three commissions focus on the themes of sacrifice and redemption: the Virgin Mary occupies a central role in Catholic theology as an icon of salvation; Christ's Passion and suffering are the basis for devotion to the Sacred Heart of Jesus; and St Joseph is traditionally considered the patron saint of a happy death, as he died in the arms of the Virgin and Jesus following a vigil lasting nine days and nine nights. Willie Pearse's commitment to the ideologies that underpinned the 1916 Rising is mirrored by his devout Catholicism: he attended Good Friday services in the Passionist monastery of Mount Argus, Harold's Cross (where he sculpted a figure of the Virgin, and his father before him carved an altar); he received Communion at Easter Sunday Mass in St Francis Xavier Church, Gardiner Street (run by the Jesuit order which promoted devotion to the Sacred Heart); he made his Confession to Fr Richard Bowden, Administrator of St Mary's Pro-Cathedral, while barricaded into the GPO; and, finally, he received the last rites from Fr Augustine Hayden, a priest of the Capuchin order that commissioned the Sacred Heart altar in 1907. It is quite likely that as the moment of his execution approached, Willie Pearse may have had a passing thought for the altars he carved – particularly the figure of St Joseph – and that the subject matter of these commissions gave him some spiritual comfort.

NOTES

An original admission ticket to Patrick Pearse's Gaelic League lecture is included in *Inspiring Ireland* 1916, a series of exhibitions of the cultural artefacts, stories and interpretation that surround 1916, on the *Inspiring Ireland* website (www.inspiring-ireland.ie) which is powered by the preservation infrastructure of the Digital Repository of Ireland (DRI), a certified repository for Ireland's social and cultural data (www.dri.ie).

FURTHER READING

Brian Crowley, 'Pearse, William', *Irish Art and Architecture, iii: Sculpture* (Yale: Yale University Press, 2014).

William Murphy, 'Pearse, William ('Willie')', *Dictionary of Irish Biography* (Cambridge: Cambridge University Press, 2009).

Róisín Ní Ghairbhí, *16 Lives: Willie Pearse* (Dublin: The O'Brien Press, 2015).

JOSEPH PLUNKETT: MARTYRDOM AND MYSTICISM

CLODAGH TAIT

J oseph Plunkett (1887–1916) entered the 1916 Rising as a member of the IRB military council. In his case, the cause of independence was a family project. He was joined in armed rebellion by his two brothers, George Oliver and Jack, while his sisters Philomena and Geraldine were also involved in its planning and execution. His parents, George Noble Plunkett – a papal count, Director of the National Museum, and later a TD – and Josephine (née Cranny), were arrested following the Rising. The story of Joseph Plunkett's marriage to his 'tragic bride', Grace Gifford, in his prison cell in Kilmainham hours before his execution became one of the Rising's most romanticised episodes.

One of Count Plunkett's proudest boasts was his collateral descent from Oliver Plunkett (1625–81), Catholic Archbishop of Armagh, who was executed at Tyburn in 1681 during the Titus Oates plot. Interest in Plunkett's cult had been revived in the nineteenth century, especially by Patrick Francis Moran's biography of 1861, and by the introduction of Plunkett's cause for canonisation in 1886. Count and Countess Plunkett became the main agitators for the advancement of Oliver's cause in Rome. As early as 1904, the Count appeared before the committee compiling evidence to inform the process for the beatification of nearly three hundred early modern Irish martyrs. Indeed, the cause of Oliver Plunkett was indirectly co-opted by Joseph in 1915, when his journey to New York to meet with the leaders of Clan na Gael was disguised as a trip to meet with his mother who was then in the USA, apparently (according to John Devoy [1842–1928]) to raise funds for Oliver's beatification. Their mother's extended stay in America also provided cover for Philomena Plunkett's trips across the Atlantic in 1915 and 1916, carrying letters between Devoy and the military council. After Joseph's death, Oliver Plunkett's beatification in 1920 became a serious propaganda coup for both Count Plunkett and his Sinn Féin colleagues when Pope Benedict XV prayed that Ireland 'may obtain what she legitimately longs for' – an overt expression of support for independence.

Joseph was not officially allowed into the US during his 1915 trip, and was only permitted to stay in New York for two months when Devoy paid a bond of one thousand dollars. From the age of two he had suffered from tuberculosis of the lymph glands. It was a diagnosis that he and his family would have been reluctant to admit to, given the stigma surrounding TB at the time – it seems that even Grace Gifford was not told the extent of his illness. By Easter 1916 Joseph's health was failing. A few days before the Rising he underwent an operation on an abscess on his neck and doctors had given him weeks to live. It may be that Plunkett's anxiety that the Rising go ahead despite the countermanding order stemmed from the knowledge that he would be unable to participate in any later action.

During his days in the GPO and Kilmainham, Plunkett's equanimity and humour in the face of ill-health were commented on by many who met him. His last words, spoken to Fr Sebastian O'Brien OFM Cap., were 'Father,

I am very happy. I am dying for the glory of God and the honour of Ireland.' He had used the second sentence before, in Germany, in a declaration to be sworn by recruits to the Irish Brigade of POWs Roger Casement was putting together. A number of the other leaders likewise spoke of their belief in the need to revive Ireland's lost honour. But there was also a depth of meaning in Plunkett's understanding of dying 'for the glory of God', and in his expressions of happiness to Fr Sebastian and also in a letter to Grace Gifford. Plunkett, in his extensive reading on Christian mysticism, came to understand the things of the world as expressions of the glory of God. Such ideas appear frequently in his poetry. A few months before his death he wrote to Grace Gifford of 'seeing his glory in the beauty of the things he created and especially through your love for me and mine for you'. In the same letter he argued that Christ:

> Suffered shameful torture and death on the cross that we might see and know what was right to choose and choose the right by our free will when it would be the most difficult. I am prepared to act on those beliefs and follow him in the most difficult way for love. I am ready to go into darkness, danger and death trusting in his love that the issue will be joy.

The works on mysticism he had read, such as those by Evelyn Underhill and others mentioned in a letter of February 1916, spoke of the glory of God being expressed through action (including 'heroic action' as a 'leader of men'). Underhill also discussed in detail the notion of the 'Unitive Life' –

'the life in which man's will is united with God' – and the 'gaiety, freedom, assurance, and joy' flowing from it. 'The spirit of man having at last come to full consciousness of reality, completes the circle of Being; and returns to fertilise those levels of existence from which it sprang.' Such ideas undoubtedly both informed Plunkett's justification of violent insurrection and also shaped his actions and demeanour in his last days.

FURTHER READING

John Devoy, *Recollections of an Irish Rebel* (New York: Chas D. Young, 1929).

Patrick Francis Moran, *Memoirs of the Most Reverend Oliver Plunkett* (Dublin: James Duffy, 1861 and Dublin: Brown and Nolan, 1895).

Honor Ó Brolcháin, *16 Lives: Joseph Plunkett* (Dublin: The O'Brien Press, 2012).

Evelyn Underhill, *Mysticism* (London: Methuen, 1911).

LIST OF CONTRIBUTORS

GEARÓID BARRY is Lecturer (above the bar) in History at the National University of Ireland, Galway.

DAMIEN BURKE is Assistant Archivist at the Irish Jesuit Archives.

CATRIONA CROWE is a genealogist and Manager of Limerick Genealogy, a professional genealogical research service for Limerick, established in 2006.

BERNIE DEASY is Archivist at the Delany Archive, which cares for the archival collections of the Diocese of Kildare and Leighlin, the Patrician Brothers, Brigidine Sisters and Carlow College.

NOELLE DOWLING is Archivist at Dublin Diocesan Archives.

RODDY HEGARTY is Director of the Cardinal Tomás Ó Fiaich Memorial Library and Archive.

LIAM IRWIN is Retired Head of the Department of History, Mary Immaculate College, University of Limerick.

BRIAN KIRBY is Archivist at the Irish Capuchin Provincial Archives.

BARBARA MCCORMACK is Special Collections Librarian at Maynooth University and St Patrick's College, Maynooth.

CAROLINE MCGEE is Project Creative Lead for *Inspiring Ireland 1916* at the Digital Repository of Ireland.

JOSEPH MACMAHON OFM is Secretary of the Franciscan Province of Ireland.

GERARD MCNAMEE is Archivist and Teacher of History and Classics (recently retired), St Malachy's College, Belfast.

DAICHI Ó CORRÁIN is Lecturer in History at St Patrick's College, Dublin City University.

CONN Ó MAOLDHOMHNAIGH is a priest of the Diocese of Kildare and Leighlin and President of St Patrick's College, Carlow.

GEARÓID Ó CUACHAIGH is Emeritus Professor of History at National University of Ireland, Galway.

OLIVER RAFFERTY SJ is Professor of History and Director of Irish Programs, Boston College.

SALVADOR RYAN is Professor of Ecclesiastical History at St Patrick's College, Maynooth.

CLODAGH TAIT is Lecturer in History at Mary Immaculate College, University of Limerick.

ACKNOWLEDGEMENTS

Heartfelt thanks are due in the first instance to Dr Brendan Leahy, Bishop of Limerick, who instigated the project and offered every support at each stage of the endeavour. Sincere thanks are also due to each of the eighteen contributors who responded so willingly to the invitation to contribute to the volume. It was particularly heartening to receive the many contributions from archivists working in the area of Church archives both in diocesan archives and the archives of religious congregations. I wish to thank the following individuals and institutions for permission to allow images to be reproduced here: Bernie Deasy, archivist, Delany Archive; Brian Hodkinson, curator, Limerick Museum; Brian Kirby, archivist, Irish Capuchin Provincial Archives; Barbara McCormack, special collections librarian, Maynooth University and St Patrick's College, Maynooth; Caroline McGee; Kilmainham Gaol Museum; Limerick Diocesan Archive; Pearse Museum, St Enda's Park, Rathfarnham. Thanks also to Dr Donal Murray, bishop emeritus, and to Dr Úna Ní Bhroiméil of Mary Immaculate College, University of Limerick, for their help and encouragement. Finally, I would like to express my sincere gratitude to the staff at Veritas Publications, in particular Donna Doherty, Emma O'Donoghue, Barbara Croatto and Pamela McLoughlin, for bringing this volume to completion.